THE HONOR OF THE TOWEL

Embracing the Call,
Carrying the Weight,
Serving with Integrity

Erick D. Bowens

THE HONOR OF THE TOWEL

Embracing the Call, Carrying the Weight, Serving with Integrity

Published by Bowens Publishing House

ISBN: 979-8-9909121-9-9

Printed in the United States of America

DEDICATION

To every leader, mentor, and voice
God placed in my life to shape me,
correct me and develop me.

To those who taught me that faithfulness matters more
than visibility, and that serving well
is the foundation of leading well.
Because of you, I learned that
excellence is the standard—not the goal.
And because of that… I am better.

TABLE OF CONTENTS

INTRODUCTION

BEFORE YOU TURN THE PAGE

This is not a book you read and move on from.
This is a book that reads you back.
Because everything in these pages will do one of two things:

- **Confirm where you are**
- **Confront where you are not**

And you need both.

Why This Book Exists

There is a gap in the church.
Not a gap in talent.
Not a gap in passion.
Not even a gap in calling.
There is a gap in **alignment**.
We have:

- gifted people without discipline
- called people without clarity
- serving people without consistency
- leaders without structure

And the result is confusion, frustration, and stagnation.
Not because people don't love God...
But because they don't understand **how to function in what He's building**.
This book exists to close that gap.

This Will Challenge You

If you're looking for something that:

- makes you feel good
- agrees with everything you're doing
- avoids uncomfortable truths

This is not that.

This will challenge:

- your habits
- your mindset
- your consistency

- your motives

Because growth does not happen through comfort.
It happens through **confrontation and correction**.

This Is About Responsibility, Not Recognition

This book will not teach you how to:

- get a platform
- gain a title
- be seen

It will teach you how to:

- be trusted
- be consistent
- be aligned
- carry responsibility

Because in the Kingdom:

👉 Visibility is not the goal

👉 **Trust is**

You Will See Yourself in This Book

At some point, you will read something and think:
"That's me."
Don't skip it.
Don't defend it.
Don't explain it away.
Sit with it.
Because that moment is where change begins.

This Only Works If You Respond

You can read every chapter.
Highlight every line.
Agree with every point.
And still not change.
Because knowledge does not produce transformation.

👉 **Application does**

So don't just read this.
Respond to it.

Before You Go Further

Ask yourself one question:

Am I ready to be challenged—or do I just want to be affirmed?

Because your answer to that question
will determine what this book does for you.

CHAPTER 1

FAITHFULNESS

BEFORE LEADERSHIP

Why God Trusts Consistency

Before He Releases Responsibility

Before God gives a platform, He looks for faithfulness.
Before He entrusts influence, He examines consistency.
Before He allows someone to lead publicly, He watches how they live privately.
This is the order of the Kingdom, and it does not bend for gifting, charisma, talent, personality, or potential.
Many people desire leadership. Few understand what qualifies it.
In the world, leadership is often built on visibility, confidence, and opportunity. If someone is gifted enough, connected enough, attractive enough, articulate enough, or popular enough, doors may open for them. But the Kingdom of God does not build leadership that way.
In the Kingdom, leadership is built on something less flashy and far more demanding.
Faithfulness.
Faithfulness is not dramatic. It does not always get noticed. It does not always feel rewarding. It does not always come with applause, affirmation, or immediate opportunity. But faithfulness is the foundation of everything God can trust.
Jesus said:

> ***Luke 16:10 (NLT)***
> *"If you are faithful in little things, you will be faithful in large ones. But if you are dishonest in little things, you won't be honest with greater responsibilities."*

That verse destroys the illusion that people are suddenly ready for greater weight simply because they desire it.
God does not guess who can handle more.
He watches how they handle what they already have.
A person does not become faithful when they receive a title. A title only reveals what was already there. If inconsistency was present before the title, the title will not cure it. If poor stewardship was present before the position, the position will not fix it. If a person was unreliable before responsibility, more responsibility will only expose the unreliability at a higher level.
God does not test your calling with opportunity first.
He tests it with consistency.

Faithfulness Begins in the Quiet Places

Faithfulness is proven in places most people never see.
It is proven when you show up and no one claps.
It is proven when you serve and no one says your name.
It is proven when you give and no one knows what it cost you.
It is proven when you remain committed after the excitement wears off.
It is proven when you do what you said you would do, even when it is no longer convenient.
That is where leadership begins.
Leadership does not begin when a title is announced.
Leadership begins when responsibility is accepted.
Long before someone is recognized as a deacon, minister, elder, evangelist, missionary, pastor, overseer, or bishop, they must first become faithful.
Faithfulness is not the decoration of leadership.

Faithfulness is the foundation of leadership.
Without it, everything else eventually cracks.

Private Faithfulness Comes Before Public Responsibility

One of the greatest mistakes in church culture is celebrating public ability before examining private consistency.
A person can be gifted and still be unstable.
A person can be articulate and still be unreliable.
A person can be passionate and still be unprepared.
A person can love the microphone and still not love responsibility.
That is why faithfulness must come first.
God does not release public weight without first examining private patterns.
How do you handle what no one sees?
How do you respond when no one checks on you?
How do you serve when no one thanks you?
How do you give when no one is watching?
How do you follow through when no one is forcing you?
These questions matter because private patterns always become public problems when they are not corrected.
If someone is inconsistent privately, public leadership will not make them consistent. It will only give their inconsistency more people to affect.

Faithfulness in Stewardship

One of the clearest places faithfulness shows up is in stewardship.

How you handle your time, commitments, assignments, money, presence, attitude, and follow-through reveals what you actually value.

This is why giving cannot be treated like a side issue in leadership development.

It is not a side issue.

It is a spiritual issue, a biblical issue, and a structure issue.

Scripture says:

> ***Malachi 3:10 (NKJV)***
>
> *"Bring all the tithes into the storehouse, that there may be food in My house, and try Me now in this," says the Lord of hosts, "If I will not open for you the windows of heaven and pour out for you such blessing that there will not be room enough to receive it."*

Tithing is not merely a financial habit. It is a declaration of trust.

It says:

God is my source.

I honor His Word.

I support His house.

I am committed to what feeds me spiritually.

A person cannot claim devotion to the house while refusing to support it faithfully. That contradiction eventually shows up in how they serve.

When leaders faithfully support the house of God with their resources, time, presence, and participation, they demonstrate something deeper than generosity. They demonstrate alignment.

They are saying, "I am not just benefiting from this house. I am helping carry it."

That matters.

Because leadership is not just about what you say you love.

Leadership is about what you help sustain.

Ministry Must Never Contradict the Message

Years ago, Bishop Mark Tolbert asked me a question that cut deeper than I expected.

He asked, "Are you a preacher?"

I answered, "Yes."

He said, "You can't be, because how can you stand up, preach the Bible, which is truth, and not live by what the Bible of truth says? If you're not consistently sowing, you're not living what you preach."

That statement exposed something many people avoid:

Ministry must never contradict the message.

If we preach faith, we must live by faith.

If we preach obedience, we must walk in obedience.

If we preach giving, we must be givers.

If we preach commitment, we must be committed.

If we preach faithfulness, we must be faithful.

Otherwise, we are speaking truth we are unwilling to practice.

And truth preached without personal alignment eventually loses credibility.

The credibility of leadership begins with integrity.

Paul wrote:

1 Corinthians 4:2 (NLT)

"Now, a person who is put in charge as a manager must be faithful."

Not impressive.

Not talented.

Not charismatic.

Faithful.

That word cuts through everything.

Because gifting may open a door, but faithfulness determines whether you can be trusted to stay there.

Faithfulness in Pressure

Faithfulness is easy to claim when life is calm.

But pressure reveals what commitment is really made of.

Anybody can be faithful when the schedule is light, the emotions are high, the opportunity is fresh, and the assignment feels exciting.

But what happens when life gets busy?

What happens when the assignment becomes repetitive?

What happens when nobody notices?

What happens when you are tired?

What happens when your feelings are not cooperating?

What happens when you are corrected?

What happens when someone else is recognized before you?

That is where faithfulness is tested.

Not in the moment of inspiration, but in the season of inconvenience.

If your commitment disappears every time life gets heavy, then your commitment was never fully established. It was conditional.
And conditional faithfulness is not faithfulness.

Faithfulness in Delay

Faithfulness is also tested in delay.
Many people can serve as long as they believe elevation is coming quickly. But when time passes and the title does not come, the opportunity does not open, or the recognition does not happen, their heart begins to shift.
They still serve, but now with irritation.
They still show up, but now with resentment.
They still participate, but now with comparison.
That is dangerous.
Because delay does not only reveal patience.
Delay reveals motive.
If the only reason you served was because you thought it would get you promoted, then you were not serving. You were negotiating.
True faithfulness does not use service as a transaction.
True faithfulness says, "God, I will honor You here, whether this leads to visibility or not."
That kind of faithfulness can be trusted.

Faithfulness in Correction

Another place faithfulness is tested is correction.
Many people are faithful until they are corrected.
They can serve as long as they are celebrated.
They can follow as long as they agree.
They can be committed as long as no one challenges them.
But correction reveals whether a person is truly submitted or simply involved.
A faithful person can be corrected without disappearing.
A faithful person can be challenged without becoming offended.
A faithful person can receive adjustment without treating it like rejection.
This matters because leadership requires growth, and growth requires correction.
If you cannot be corrected, you cannot be developed.
And if you cannot be developed, you cannot be trusted with greater responsibility.

The Church Must Stop Promoting Potential Without Proving Patterns

Too often, churches train people before testing their consistency.
They develop voices before examining stewardship.
They hand out responsibility before confirming reliability.
Then later they discover:
The person is not a faithful giver.
The person is not consistent in attendance.
The person is not dependable in service.
The person loves the title more than the responsibility.
The person wants visibility without accountability.

At that point, the issue is not gifting.

The issue is foundation.

And if the foundation is weak, the structure will eventually show cracks.

This is not harsh.

It is biblical.

God does not lower His standards to accommodate someone's potential.

He develops people until they can carry His standards with integrity.

Faithfulness is not punishment.

Faithfulness is preparation.

It is God's way of strengthening what He plans to use.

Desire Is Not Readiness

Before anyone is trusted with greater responsibility, they must answer honestly:

Am I faithful right now?

Not:

Do I feel called?

Do I have potential?

Do I want to serve?

Do people think I am gifted?

But:

Am I consistent?

Am I dependable?

Am I supporting the house of God?

Am I present?

Am I teachable?

Am I living what I say I believe?
Because until faithfulness is established, everything else is premature.
Desire is not readiness.
Potential is not proof.
Gifting is not government.
Calling is not a substitute for consistency.
The question is not, "Can God use me?"
Of course He can.
The question is, "Can I be trusted with what God wants to use me for?"

Real-Life Ministry Scenario

You committed to serve.
At first, you were excited. You were available, eager, responsive, and ready to help.
Then life got busy.
You did not completely disappear, but you became less dependable. You still see yourself as committed, but your patterns tell a different story.
You show up when it works for you.
You give when it is comfortable.
You serve when it does not interfere with what you would rather do.
You respond when you feel like it.
You follow through when someone reminds you.
No one has confronted you yet, so you have convinced yourself that everything is fine.
But here is the real question:

At what point did your commitment become conditional? Because conditional faithfulness is not faithfulness.

Self-Evaluation

Answer these honestly:

1. Where am I inconsistent right now?
2. Do I only show up when it is convenient?
3. Am I a faithful and consistent tither and giver?
4. Does my attendance reflect commitment or preference?
5. If leadership tracked my consistency for the last three months, what would it reveal?
6. Am I asking for responsibility that my current habits do not support?
7. Do I receive correction well, or do I become distant when challenged?
8. What part of my life says, "I'm committed," and what part says otherwise?

Check Your Heart

Be honest before God:

Am I faithful, or am I just available when it works for me?

Do I want the honor of leadership more than the discipline that prepares me for it?

Have I mistaken desire for readiness?

Am I supporting the house, or simply benefiting from it?

Have I allowed delay to change my attitude?

Do I become offended when accountability exposes inconsistency?

This is where excuses die.

Action Assignment

Do not just agree with this chapter.

Respond to it.

Write down one area where you have been inconsistent:

- giving
- attendance
- service
- prayer
- follow-through
- communication
- preparation
- accountability

Correct it immediately.

Not next month.

Not when life slows down.

Now.

Track that one area for the next seven days.

If needed, acknowledge the inconsistency to someone in leadership or to someone who can hold you accountable.

Then write and repeat this commitment:

I will not pursue leadership while ignoring faithfulness.

Now that the foundation is clear, the next question is not whether leadership matters.

The next question is what leadership is supposed to look like in the Kingdom of God.

Because God did not define leadership the way people do.

He did not begin with a platform.

He did not begin with a title.

He did not begin with a microphone.

He defined it with something unexpected.

A towel.

CHAPTER 2
THE HONOR OF THE TOWEL

When Jesus Redefined Leadership Forever

If you misunderstand leadership, you will misuse authority.
And if you misuse authority, you will damage people.
That is why Jesus did not assume His disciples understood leadership.
He redefined it in front of them.
Not with a sermon.
Not with a title.
Not with a position.
But with a towel.

The Moment Most People Read Too Fast

John 13:3–5 (NLT)

3 Jesus knew that the Father had given him authority over everything and that he had come from God and would return to God. 4 So he got up from the table, took off his robe, wrapped a towel around his waist, 5 and poured water into a basin. Then he began to wash the disciples' feet, drying them with the towel he had around him.

Jesus knew that the Father had given Him authority over everything.
He knew where He came from.
He knew where He was going.
And with full awareness of His authority...
He got up from the table.
Wrapped a towel around His waist.
Poured water into a basin.
And began washing the disciples' feet.

Slow that down.

This was not random.

This was intentional.

Because in that moment, Jesus was not just serving.

He was correcting a mindset.

What the Disciples Were Thinking

Before this moment, the disciples had been arguing about rank.

Who would be the greatest?

Who would be closest?

Who would matter most?

And while they were thinking about position…

Jesus picked up a towel.

Here is the uncomfortable truth:

The job of washing feet was already assigned in that culture.

But nobody did it.

Why?

Because it was beneath them.

So they sat there…

waiting for someone else to do what they all knew needed to be done.

And Jesus addressed it without a speech.

He addressed it with action.

The Towel Was Not Low—It Was Revealing

Foot washing was not symbolic.

It was practical.

It was uncomfortable.

It was humbling.

It was assigned to the lowest servant in the room.

And Jesus chose it.

Not because He lacked authority.

But because He had it.

That changes everything.

Because insecurity avoids service.

But true authority is not threatened by it.

Leadership Is Not Position—It Is Responsibility

The towel represents:

Responsibility

Humility

Awareness

Availability

Willingness to do what others avoid

Leadership is not:

Being seen

Being heard

Being followed

Leadership is:

Taking responsibility for what others overlook

You Cannot Skip the Towel

Many people want influence.

Few want responsibility.

They want to lead...

But they do not want to serve.

They want visibility...

But they avoid what is inconvenient.

But in the Kingdom:

You cannot carry authority

if you have never carried a towel.

Because the towel teaches you:

Patience

Discipline

Sensitivity to people

Attention to detail

Consistency without recognition

Without those things...

Leadership becomes dangerous.

Serving What You Didn't Create

This is where many people fail.

They want ownership

before stewardship.

They want influence

before responsibility.

They want to lead

what they have not proven they can support.

But the Kingdom requires something different.

Serve what exists

before you try to lead what's next.

Because if you cannot honor what is already built...

You are not ready to build anything new.

This shows up in real ways:

You critique what you have not carried.

You question what you have not supported.

You want to change what you have not understood.

And now instead of strengthening the house...

You become a source of tension inside of it.

Serving what you did not create is not weakness.

It is maturity.

The Towel Exposes Your Motive

Service reveals things preaching cannot hide.

It reveals:

Your attitude

Your patience

Your pride

Your expectations

Your entitlement

Because when you are serving:

There is no stage to perform on

There is no microphone to hide behind

There is no applause to sustain you

There is only your heart

And your consistency

The towel will quietly confront what you would rather ignore.

Authority and Humility Are Not Opposites

John 13:13–14 (NLT)

"You call me 'Teacher' and 'Lord,' and you are right, because that's what I am. And since I, your Lord and Teacher, have washed your feet, you ought to wash each other's feet."

Jesus did not deny His authority.

He demonstrated how it should function.

True authority does not demand service.

It models it.

The Discipline of Seeing Needs

One of the most overlooked parts of leadership is awareness.

Jesus saw what nobody addressed.

That is leadership.

Not waiting to be told.

Not waiting to be asked.

Seeing what needs to be done

and taking responsibility for it.

Most people see problems.

Few people take ownership.

Leaders do not wait.

They respond.

The Weight of the Towel

Service is not light.

It carries weight.

You carry:

People

Problems

Pressure

Expectations

And you carry them without always being acknowledged.

That is why the towel is not just a symbol of humility.

It is a symbol of responsibility.

The Towel Never Comes Off

Here is where many people misunderstand leadership.

They think the towel is temporary.

Something you use until you get promoted.

But in the Kingdom...

The higher you go

The tighter the towel should be.

Because leadership never outgrows service.

It deepens it.

The Question You Must Answer

Are you willing to carry the towel:

When it is unseen?

When it is uncomfortable?

When it is inconvenient?

When it is not reciprocated?

When no one thanks you?

Because that answer reveals more about your readiness than your gifting ever will.

Real-Life Ministry Scenario

You have been serving faithfully.

Showing up.

Helping.

Supporting.

Carrying weight behind the scenes.

Then suddenly...

Someone else gets elevated.

Someone else gets recognized.

Someone else gets the opportunity you thought you were next for.

And now something shifts.

You still serve.

But not the same.

There is tension.

Frustration.

Quiet comparison.

👉 The real question:

Did your assignment change... or did your heart change?

Self-Evaluation

Be honest:

Do I serve the same when no one acknowledges me?

Do I get frustrated when others are elevated before me?

Have I ever thought something was beneath me?

Do I struggle serving what I didn't build?

If nobody ever saw what I do... would I still do it?

Check Your Heart

Am I serving for God—or for recognition?

Has my attitude shifted because I feel overlooked?

Do I carry responsibility—or expectation?

Have I confused serving with earning a position?

Do I want the platform more than the towel?

Action Assignment

Identify one area where your service has become conditional.

Reset your posture immediately—no announcement needed.

Serve in a hidden way this week (something no one will see).

Take responsibility for something you previously ignored.

Write and declare:

I will carry the towel with the right heart—whether I am seen or not.

Now we have established two things:

Faithfulness qualifies you.

Servanthood defines you.

But here is the next tension.

You can be faithful.

You can serve.

And still not understand your calling.

That is where confusion begins.

So next... we deal with clarity.

Because everyone is called.

But not everyone understands how.

CHAPTER 3

EVERYONE IS CALLED

But Not Everyone Is Assigned the Same Way

There is a dangerous assumption that quietly lives in the church:
Only certain people are called.
The ones with microphones.
The ones with titles.
The ones with visible roles.
Everyone else?
They are just "members."
That thinking is not only inaccurate.
It is unbiblical.

Calling Is Not Selective—It Is Specific

Romans 11:29 (NKJV)
"For the gifts and the calling of God are irrevocable."
If you belong to God, you are called by God.
Not randomly.
Not emotionally.
Specifically.
The real issue is not whether you are called.
The issue is whether you understand your calling—
or whether you are trying to imitate someone else's.

The Lie That Creates Frustration

Here is the lie:
"If I am called, I should be seen."
That lie produces frustration, comparison, and quiet resentment.
Because now your measurement for calling becomes:
Who is preaching
Who is leading

Who is recognized

Who is platformed

And when that is your measurement, you will always feel overlooked.

Because you are measuring visibility...

instead of alignment.

Here is the truth:

You don't just want to be used.

You want to be seen.

And until that is confronted, your calling will always be in conflict with your expectations.

Calling, Assignment, and Office Are Not the Same

This is where most people get off track.

Let's make it plain.

Calling

Your divine purpose.

What God has wired you to carry.

Assignment

Where and who that calling is directed toward.

Office

A recognized role within the structure of the church.

Here is the problem:

People feel a calling...

and immediately assume they are supposed to step into an office.

So they skip:

Development

Submission

Faithfulness

Process

And try to step into something they have not been prepared to carry.

That creates confusion.

Because calling without development produces pressure you cannot sustain.

You Can Be Called and Still Be in Process

Moses was called in Exodus 3…

but did not immediately lead a nation.

David was anointed king…

but went back to tending sheep.

Jesus was the Son of God…

and still submitted to process before public ministry.

Calling does not mean ready.

Calling means responsible to develop.

God does not rush what He plans to trust.

He develops it.

He stretches it.

He proves it.

Over time.

What Happens When You Move Too Fast

Let's be honest.

You can preach and not be called to preach.

You can lead and not be assigned to lead.

You can speak and not be ready to speak.

And when that happens, you don’t produce impact.

You produce confusion.

Because calling is not about what you can do.

It is about what you are aligned to do.

Ability without alignment is dangerous.

Because it creates influence without foundation.

And influence without foundation always collapses.

Everyone Is Called—But Not to the Same Thing

1 Corinthians 12:18 (CSB)

“But as it is, God has arranged each one of the parts in the body just as he wanted.”

That means:

Some are visible.

Some are behind the scenes.

Some lead publicly.

Some strengthen privately.

But all are necessary.

The problem is not calling.

The problem is comparison.

Because comparison will make you:

Despise your role

Minimize your impact

Chase what was never assigned to you

And ignore what God is already trusting you with.

Your Calling Will Always Be Connected to People

God never calls you in isolation.

He calls you to people.

That means your calling will show up in:

Who you are drawn to

Who you feel a burden for

Who you naturally connect with

Who your story resonates with

And here is the part many people avoid:

Most times, the people you are called to

look like your past.

Your struggles.

Your mistakes.

Your growth.

That is not coincidence.

That is preparation.

Your Pain Is Not Random—It Is Preparation

The thing you wanted to hide…

God often wants to use.

What you survived

What you overcame

What you learned

Becomes the bridge between you and the people you are assigned to.

Because people don't just respond to information.

They respond to authenticity.

They respond to truth that has been lived.

They respond to someone who understands.

If you hide your story…

You hide your impact.

The Danger of Waiting for a Moment

Many people are waiting for an opportunity.

A microphone.

A platform.

A title.

Something official.

And until that happens, they stay passive.

But here is the truth:

You are already in position.

You already have access.

You already have influence.

You already have people.

You just have not acknowledged it.

Because you are waiting for a moment…

instead of responding to responsibility.

Calling Without Faithfulness Will Frustrate You

Let's bring this back to foundation.

You can:

Feel called

Know you are called

Be confident you are called

But if you are not faithful…

that calling will never mature into responsibility.

Instead, it will produce:

Frustration

Comparison

Disconnection

Because you will feel like you are supposed to be doing more... while ignoring what you have been given now.

The Question You Must Answer

Not:

"Am I called?"

But:

"Am I submitted to the process that develops my calling?"

Because calling without development leads to frustration.

And frustration leads to:

Comparison

Competition

Disconnection

Closing Thought

Everyone is called.

But not everyone:

Understands their calling

Submits to their calling

Develops their calling

And until you do...

You will spend your life trying to be something instead of becoming what God designed.

Real-Life Ministry Scenario

You feel called.

You know there is more in you.

You feel the pull to teach, to lead, to speak, to impact lives.

But nothing has opened yet.

No platform.

No microphone.

No official opportunity.

So you wait.

Meanwhile:

You pass up conversations where you could speak life.

You stay quiet when you know you should say something.

You overlook people God keeps putting in front of you.

And without realizing it, you have made a decision:

"I will walk in my calling when my opportunity comes."

👉 The real question:

Are you waiting for an opportunity... or ignoring your assignment?

Self-Evaluation

Be honest:

Do I associate my calling with a platform or position?

Am I waiting to be recognized before I act?

Who am I currently influencing right now?

Have I overlooked opportunities because they felt too small?

Do I consistently use my voice where I already have access?

Check Your Heart

Do I want to be seen more than I want to serve?
Have I become frustrated because I am not "up yet"?
Am I comparing my journey to someone else's calling?
Have I ignored the people God already placed in my life?
Do I truly care about people—or just purpose?

Action Assignment

Write down the names of 2–3 people currently in your life you can intentionally impact.
Identify one conversation this week where you will speak life, truth, or encouragement.
Use your current environment as your pulpit (home, work, friendships).
Stop waiting for recognition—start responding to responsibility.
Write out your "burning bush moment":
When did something first stir in you?
What has God consistently placed on your heart?
What have you been ignoring or delaying?

Now that you understand that everyone has a calling…
and that your calling is connected to people…
we must take the next step.
Because if you are called…
and if you already have people…
then you already have something else.
A place where your voice is meant to be used.
A pulpit.

CHAPTER 4

EVERYONE HAS A PULPIT

Your Life Is Already Speaking

Whether You Realize It or Not

Most people think a pulpit is a place.
A stage.
A platform.
A microphone.
A Sunday morning moment.
But in the Kingdom of God, a pulpit is not furniture.
It is influence.

The Misunderstanding That Creates Passivity

Because people define a pulpit as a stage...
They disconnect from responsibility.
They assume:
"If I'm not preaching, I'm not leading."
"If I don't have a mic, I don't have impact."
"If I'm not up front, I'm not being used."
That mindset is wrong.
And it creates passive believers who are waiting for visibility instead of walking in responsibility.

Jesus Already Settled This

> *Matthew 5:14–16 (NLT)*
> *"You are the light of the world... let your good deeds shine out for all to see, so that everyone will praise your heavenly Father."*

Notice what Jesus did NOT say.
He did not say:
Preachers are the light.
Leaders are the light.

Those with titles are the light.

He said:

YOU are the light.

That means:

If you belong to God, you carry influence.

Not later.

Now.

Your Life Is Already Preaching

You don't start influencing people when you get a platform.

You've been influencing people.

By how you live.

By how you respond.

By what you tolerate.

By how you handle pressure.

By how you treat people.

By what you prioritize.

Your life is already communicating something.

The real question is:

What is it saying?

A Pulpit Is Any Place You Shape Lives

Your pulpit may not be public—but it is still powerful.

It may look like:

A conversation at work

A group chat

A classroom

A family environment

A friendship circle
A quiet moment where someone is watching how you respond
Wherever your life has the ability to shape someone else—
That is your pulpit.

Stop Waiting for Permission to Be Responsible

One of the most limiting mindsets people carry is this:
"I'll take responsibility when I'm given a role."
But responsibility does not begin with a role.
It begins with awareness.
If God has placed you somewhere...
He expects you to represent Him there.
Not later.
Now.

The Danger of Waiting to Be Seen

Many people delay growth because they are waiting to be recognized.
They think:
"When I get the opportunity..."
"When I get put up..."
"When they notice me..."
Then they will step into responsibility.
But here is the reality:
If you are not faithful in your current pulpit...
You are not ready for a bigger one.
God does not increase visibility to create faithfulness.
He increases visibility because of it.

Private Influence Prepares Public Responsibility

Before David stood before Goliath...

he was alone with sheep.

Before Joseph led a nation...

he served in a prison.

Before Jesus preached publicly...

He lived quietly.

God always tests influence in private

before trusting it in public.

What Are You Teaching Without Saying a Word?

People are always learning from you.

Even when you're not speaking.

They are learning:

How to respond

How to handle conflict

How to treat people

How to carry pressure

How to prioritize God

You may not feel like a leader...

But if someone is watching you,

you are already leading.

Your Real Pulpit Is Not What You Say—It's What You Live

You can say one thing publicly...

and live something different privately.

But people don't follow your words.

They follow your patterns.

That is why integrity matters.

Because your real pulpit
is your consistency.

You Represent More Than Yourself

2 Corinthians 5:20 (NLT)
"So we are Christ's ambassadors; God is making his appeal through us."

That means:
Your actions reflect Him
Your attitude reflects Him
Your decisions reflect Him
You carry His name into every space you enter.
That is not pressure.
That is responsibility.

You Cannot Separate Your Life From Your Influence

Some people try to divide their lives:
"Church me"
"Work me"
"Private me"
But influence does not work like that.
People experience one version of you.
And that version is shaping their perception of:
God
Faith
Leadership
Integrity
Whether you realize it or not.

The Weight of Being Watched

You may never know:

Who is observing your consistency

Who is encouraged by your discipline

Who is strengthened by your faith

Who is learning from your example

But they are.

That is the weight of influence.

Holy Reverence vs. Unprepared Nerves

There will be moments where your pulpit becomes visible.

You are asked to speak.

To lead.

To teach.

To step up.

And you feel it:

Your nerves are high.

Your thoughts feel scattered.

Your body feels the weight of the moment.

Most people say:

"I'm just nervous."

But let's correct that.

There is a difference between:

Unprepared nerves

and

Holy reverence.

Unprepared nerves say:

"I didn't study enough."

"I'm not ready."

"I'm unsure."

Holy reverence says:

"I prepared."

"I studied."

"I prayed."

"But I still need God."

One is fear.

The other is awareness.

Awareness that:

This matters.

God is involved.

This is bigger than me.

That feeling is not something to eliminate.

It is something to respect.

The Question You Must Answer

Not:

"Do I have a pulpit?"

But:

"What am I doing with the one I already have?"

Because ignoring your current influence
will disqualify you from future responsibility.

Closing Thought

You don't have to wait to be used by God.

You already are.

The question is whether you are:

Intentional

Faithful

Aware

Because your life is speaking every day.

And whatever it is saying...

Someone is listening.

Real-Life Ministry Scenario

You finally get the opportunity.

You are asked to speak.

Teach.

Lead something.

This is what you have been waiting for.

But when the moment comes...

You feel it.

You are scattered.

Unclear.

Trying to pull thoughts together in real time.

Now you are asking:

"Why am I so nervous?"

 The real question:

Did you respect the moment... or assume you could carry it without preparation?

Self-Evaluation

Be honest:

Did I truly prepare, or did I assume I could "just flow"?

Did I study myself full before stepping up?

Did I take time to think myself clear?

Did I pray until I felt spiritually aligned—or just mentally ready?

Do I rely more on my ability or on God's presence?

Check Your Heart

Am I chasing moments to be seen, or moments to serve?

Do I respect the weight of standing before people?

Have I taken preparation lightly because I'm gifted?

Do I fear people's opinions more than I honor God's presence?

Action Assignment

Before your next opportunity to speak, teach, or lead:

Study yourself full.

Know your material, scripture, and flow.

Think yourself clear.

Remove clutter. Simplify your message.

Pray yourself hot.

Spend time with God until your heart is aligned.

Then let yourself go.

Trust God in the moment—don't over-control it.

Write this posture down:

This is not pressure. This is holy reverence. I am prepared, but I still need God.

Now that you understand:

You have a calling.

You have a pulpit.

And you must be prepared to carry it.

We must now go deeper into structure.

Because calling without order...

and influence without understanding...

will always create confusion.

CHAPTER 5
YOUR BURNING BUSH MOMENT

When Calling Becomes Personal, Clear, and Inescapable

There comes a moment in every person's life
where calling stops being a concept...
and becomes a confrontation.
Not emotional.
Not hype.
Not something someone else told you.
But a moment where you know:
God is speaking to me.

Moses Was Not Looking for It

> *Exodus 3:2–4 (NKJV)*
> *"The Angel of the Lord appeared to him in a flame of fire from the midst of a bush... So when the Lord saw that he turned aside to look, God called to him..."*

Moses was not in a service.
He was not at an altar.
He was not in a leadership class.
He was working.
Living.
Existing in what had become normal.
And in the middle of his routine...
God interrupted him.

Your Calling Will Interrupt Your Normal

Let's deal with this honestly.
Most people want calling...
as long as it fits their life.
But calling does not fit your life.

It confronts it.

It interrupts your comfort.

It challenges your routine.

It exposes what you have settled into.

Moses had a rhythm.

A predictable life.

And God disrupted it.

Because purpose does not ask for convenience.

It demands alignment.

The Fire Was Not the Point—The Voice Was

Many people get distracted by what they see.

The bush was burning.

But it was not consumed.

That was attention-grabbing.

But that was not the calling.

The calling happened when God spoke.

"Moses, Moses."

That is when it became personal.

Calling is not confirmed by what you see.

It is confirmed when it becomes clear that:

This is for me.

God Calls You By Name

God did not say:

"Hey you."

He said:

"Moses."

Twice.

Because calling is not generic.
It is intentional.
It is specific.
It is direct.
When God calls you, you will know.
Not because it is loud.
But because it is clear.

Before Assignment—There Was Alignment

Exodus 3:5 (NKJV)
"Do not draw near this place. Take your sandals off your feet, for the place where you stand is holy ground."
Before God told Moses what to do...
He adjusted how Moses stood.
That matters.
Because many people want assignment...
without alignment.
They want opportunity...
without reverence.
They want to move for God...
without learning how to stand before Him.
But before you move for God...
you must be aligned with Him.

Holy Reverence—Not Insecurity

This is where many people mislabel what they feel.
They say:
"I'm nervous."
"I don't know if I'm ready."

"I feel unsure."

But often, what you are feeling is not fear.

It is holy reverence.

It is the awareness that:

This matters.

God is involved.

This is bigger than me.

That tension is not always something to remove.

Sometimes it is something to respect.

Moses Tried to Talk Himself Out of It

After the encounter, Moses did not respond with confidence.

He responded with excuses.

"Who am I?"

"What if they don't believe me?"

"I'm not a good speaker."

Sound familiar?

Because when calling becomes real...

insecurity often gets louder.

Excuses Do Not Cancel Calling

Moses had a past.

He had insecurities.

He had doubt.

And none of it disqualified him.

Because calling is not based on your confidence.

It is based on God's decision.

You Don't Need to Be Ready—You Need to Be Willing

God did not fix Moses first.

He called him first.

Then developed him through the process.

That means:

You do not wait until you feel ready.

You respond when you are called.

Your Moment May Not Look Dramatic

Let's remove the fantasy.

Your burning bush moment may not look like fire.

It may not sound like an audible voice.

It may not happen in a church service.

It may look like:

A deep conviction you cannot shake

A repeated burden you cannot ignore

A persistent pull you cannot explain

A moment that keeps coming back to you

But it will be clear.

You Can Delay Calling—But You Cannot Delete It

This is where many people get stuck.

You felt it.

You knew it.

You were sure of it.

And then... you delayed.

Life got busy.

Responsibilities increased.

Distractions multiplied.

And what was once urgent…

became optional.

But calling does not disappear.

It waits.

It resurfaces.

It confronts you again.

Because God does not casually assign purpose.

If He called you…

He meant it.

What Happens When You Keep Ignoring It

Let's go deeper.

If you continue to ignore what God made clear…

it does not make you free.

It creates drift.

You begin to feel:

Disconnected

Unfulfilled

Frustrated without knowing why

Because you are living…

but not aligned.

And misalignment always creates tension.

Not because God is punishing you.

But because you are avoiding what you were created for.

What Did It Take to Get You Here?

Your calling did not start today.

It has been forming over time.

Through:

Your experiences
Your failures
Your growth
Your exposure
Your environment
Nothing you have been through is random.
It has all been preparation.

Don't Lose Your Moment

There are people who had a moment with God...
and never returned to it.
They felt it.
They acknowledged it.
But they never responded to it.
And over time...
it became a memory instead of a direction.
Do not let that be your story.

The Question You Must Answer

Not:
"Did God speak to me?"
But:
"Did I respond to what God made clear?"
Because clarity without obedience creates distance.

Closing Thought

Your burning bush moment is not about excitement.
It is about clarity.
It is the moment where you stop asking:

"Am I called?"

and start saying:

"God, I hear You."

Real-Life Ministry Scenario

You have had the moment.

Not necessarily fire in a bush...

but something undeniable.

A stirring you could not ignore.

A conviction that would not leave.

A moment where you knew:

God is trying to get my attention.

You felt it clearly.

You even told yourself:

"I need to do something about this."

But then life kept moving.

Responsibilities.

Schedules.

Distractions.

And slowly...

what was once urgent...

became optional.

Now that moment feels distant.

Not gone—but not active.

👉 The real question:

Did God stop speaking... or did you stop responding?

Self-Evaluation

Be honest:

Have I had moments where I knew God was calling me deeper?

Did I respond immediately—or delay?

What have I clearly heard from God that I have not acted on?

Have I allowed life to distract me from what God revealed?

Do I revisit what God spoke—or have I moved on from it?

Check Your Heart

Have I become comfortable ignoring what God made clear?

Do I treat divine moments as suggestions instead of instructions?

Am I waiting for confirmation when I already have clarity?

Have I allowed fear, doubt, or insecurity to delay my response?

Do I want the outcome of calling—but avoid the obedience it requires?

Action Assignment

Write down your burning bush moment in detail:

What happened?

Where were you?

What did you feel?

What did you believe God was saying?

Identify what you did after that moment:

Did you act, delay, or ignore?

Take one immediate step of obedience this week.

Remove one distraction that has pulled you away from that moment.

Write and declare:

I will not ignore what God has made clear. I will respond with obedience.

Now that you have identified:

Your calling

Your people

Your pulpit

Your defining moment

We must now prepare you properly.

Because having a calling is one thing...

But being ready to carry it is another.

CHAPTER 6
UNDERSTANDING THE HOUSE

Order, Alignment, and Why Structure Matters

You cannot serve effectively in a place
you do not understand.
Many people love the church...
But have no understanding of:
How it functions
Why it is structured the way it is
Where they fit within it
And when you do not understand structure...
you start creating your own.

God Is Not Random—He Is Intentional

1 Corinthians 14:40 (NKJV)
"Let all things be done decently and in order."
God does not build:
Without structure
Without clarity
Without alignment
Everything God establishes
has a system that supports it.
If there is no order...
there is no sustainability.

The Church Is Not an Event—It Is a Body

1 Corinthians 12:12 (NLT)
"The human body has many parts, but the many parts make up one whole body..."
The church is not just a gathering.
It is a body.

Which means:

Every part matters

Every part has function

Every part must stay aligned

A body only works

when every part knows its role

and stays in its place.

Misalignment Does Not Create Freedom—It Creates Dysfunction

If a hand tries to be a foot...

If an eye tries to be a mouth...

You do not get creativity.

You get dysfunction.

The same thing happens in the church.

When people:

Step outside their role

Ignore structure

Reject alignment

It does not create innovation.

It creates confusion.

Structure Protects What God Is Building

Some people resist structure because they think:

"Structure limits me."

No.

Structure protects:

Vision

People

Flow

Accountability

Without structure:

Everyone does what they want

No one is responsible

Nothing is sustainable

And eventually… everything breaks down.

The Flow of the House

Every healthy house has a flow.

Not control.

Flow.

Christ is the Head.

Leadership receives vision.

Structure distributes responsibility.

People execute the work.

When that flow is honored…

things move.

When it is broken…

things stall.

Authority Is Not Control—It Is Responsibility

Let's correct a dangerous mindset.

Authority is not about:

Power

Position

Being "over people"

Authority is about:

Being responsible for what God has entrusted.

That means:

Leaders carry weight

Leaders answer to God

Leaders are accountable for what happens under their care

That is not privilege.

That is responsibility.

Submission Is Not Weakness—It Is Alignment

This is where many people struggle.

Because submission has been misunderstood.

Submission is not:

Silence

Lack of voice

Blind agreement

Submission is:

Alignment with order.

Hebrews 13:17 (NKJV)

"Obey those who rule over you, and be submissive, for they watch out for your souls..."

That means:

Leadership carries responsibility for souls

And your role is to align—not compete.

You Can Be Right—and Still Be Out of Order

This is the part people do not like.

You can:

Have a good idea

See a real issue
Be passionate about change
And still be out of order.
Because in the Kingdom:
How you move
matters just as much as
what you see.
Right ideas handled wrong
create division.

Misalignment Often Sounds Like "Good Intentions"

People rarely say:
"I want to be out of order."
They say:
"I'm just trying to help."
"I see another way."
"I think this could be better."
But if it is not aligned with structure...
it creates friction.
And friction, left unchecked,
becomes division.

You Are Part of Something Bigger Than You

Your role is not about you.
It is about:
The house
The mission
The people being impacted

When you understand that…

you stop asking:

“What do I want to do?”

And start asking:

“What does the house need from me?”

Independence Is Not Maturity

Some people think growth means:

“I don’t need anybody.”

“I’ll just do it myself.”

“I’ll figure it out on my own.”

That is not maturity.

That is isolation.

And isolation leads to:

Disconnection

Error

Burnout

Maturity understands:

I am part of something.

And I function best when I am aligned.

Order Creates Clarity

When structure is clear:

People know their role

People know their responsibility

People know where to grow

When structure is unclear:

People guess

People assume
People overstep
And confusion becomes normal.

Before You Move—You Must Understand

You cannot serve well
if you do not understand where you are.
So before stepping into:
Preaching
Leading
Serving
You must understand:
The structure
The flow
The expectations

The Question You Must Answer

Not:
"Where can I fit?"
But:
"Where am I assigned—and how do I align?"

Closing Thought

The house of God is not built on talent.
It is built on:
Order
Alignment
Faithfulness

And when you understand the house...
you stop trying to create your own lane—
and start strengthening the one you have been given.

Real-Life Ministry Scenario

You are in the house.
You attend consistently.
You enjoy the Word.
You are even serving.
But over time...
You begin to feel:
Disconnected
Frustrated
Out of place
You do not fully understand:
How things function
Why decisions are made
How leadership operates
So you begin to form your own conclusions.
"I don't see why they do it like that."
"I would do it differently."
"That doesn't make sense to me."
And without realizing it...
You are in the house...
but you do not understand the house.
The real question:
Am I aligned with the house... or just attending it?

Self-Evaluation

Be honest:

Do I understand the vision of the house I am connected to?

Do I know how leadership flows and functions?

Am I aligned—or just present?

Have I taken time to learn the culture of the house?

Do I support what I do not fully understand—or resist it?

Check Your Heart

Do I honor the house—or critique it internally?

Have I allowed misunderstanding to turn into frustration?

Do I trust the leadership God has placed over the house?

Am I trying to reshape the house to fit me?

Do I see myself as a contributor—or just a consumer?

Action Assignment

Write down the vision of your house in your own words.

Identify where you currently fit within that vision.

Ask a leader for clarity in an area you do not understand.

Make a decision to align, not analyze from a distance.

Write and declare:

I will not just attend the house—I will understand, align, and support it.

Now that you understand:

Your calling

Your role

Your moment

And the house you are planted in

We must now address the structure that equips the house.

Because beyond order...

there is function.

CHAPTER 7
THE FIVE-FOLD MINISTRY

The Structure That Builds, Equips, and Stabilizes the House

The church is not sustained by activity.
It is sustained by structure and supply.
And one of the primary structures God established
to build His church
is the five-fold ministry.

This Was Not Man's Idea—It Was God's Design

> *Ephesians 4:11–12 (NKJV)*
> *"And He Himself gave some to be apostles, some prophets, some evangelists, and some pastors and teachers, for the equipping of the saints for the work of ministry, for the edifying of the body of Christ."*

Notice the language.
"He gave..."
This was not:
A church trend
A denominational structure
A leadership invention
This was a gift from Christ to the church.

The Problem: We Turn Functions into Titles

This is where things go wrong quickly.
People hear:
Apostle
Prophet
Evangelist
Pastor

Teacher

And immediately think:

Rank

Status

Position

Hierarchy

But these are not just titles.

They are functions.

And when you turn functions into titles…

you create competition instead of collaboration.

The Purpose Is Clear—But Often Ignored

"For the equipping of the saints…"

Not to impress people.

Not to build platforms.

Not to control environments.

But to:

Equip

Develop

Strengthen

Prepare

If the five-fold ministry is functioning correctly…

The people should be growing.

If Leaders Are Doing Everything—Something Is Out of Order

This is critical.

If the church depends on a few people to do everything…

Then the structure is broken.

Because leaders are not called to:

Carry everything

Do everything

Be everything

They are called to:

Equip others to function.

If people are not being developed...

Leadership is not functioning correctly.

Let's Define Each Role Clearly

No confusion. No fluff. Just function.

1. The Apostle — The Builder

The apostolic role establishes and expands.

It is concerned with:

Vision

Structure

Foundation

Expansion

The apostle:

Sees what others do not yet see

Builds systems that sustain growth

Establishes order where there is none

This is not just "starting churches."

This is building what can last.

2. The Prophet — The Aligner

The prophetic role communicates what God is saying.

It is concerned with:

Direction

Correction

Discernment

Spiritual awareness

The prophet:

Brings clarity

Exposes what is hidden

Realigns people to God's voice

But hear this clearly:

A true prophetic voice does not create confusion.

It brings alignment.

3. The Evangelist — The Gatherer

The evangelistic role brings people in.

It is concerned with:

Souls

Outreach

Expansion of people

The evangelist:

Connects with people easily

Feels urgency constantly

Carries a burden for those not yet reached

They are not satisfied with who is already in the room.

They are focused on who is missing.

4. The Pastor — The Shepherd

The pastoral role cares for people.

It is concerned with:

Growth

Protection

Stability

Development

The pastor:

Feeds

Guides

Covers

Corrects

This role is not about popularity.

It is about responsibility for people.

5. The Teacher — The Builder of Understanding

The teaching role brings clarity.

It is concerned with:

Doctrine

Understanding

Explanation

Stability through truth

The teacher:

Breaks down scripture

Explains truth clearly

Builds strong believers

Because without understanding...
people remain unstable.

These Roles Are Not Competitive—They Are Collaborative

Here is where confusion happens.
People compare roles instead of understanding them.
But the five-fold ministry is not competitive.
It is collaborative.
The apostle builds
The prophet aligns
The evangelist gathers
The pastor cares
The teacher grounds
When they work together...
The church grows:
Strong
Healthy
Balanced

Imbalance Reveals Itself Quickly

If one function dominates, problems appear.
If you only have teaching:
You get information without movement.
If you only have evangelism:
You get growth without stability.
If you only have prophetic flow:
You get revelation without structure.

If you only have pastoral care:
You get comfort without expansion.
God never intended one function
to replace the others.

Not Everyone Is Five-Fold—and That's Okay

Let's deal with this directly.
Everyone is called.
But not everyone is called to the five-fold ministry.
And that is not a limitation.
That is design.
Because the five-fold exists to equip everyone else.

You Can Carry a Grace Without Carrying the Office

You may:
Teach without being "the teacher"
Encourage without being "the pastor"
Reach people without being "the evangelist"

But office carries:
Weight
Responsibility
Accountability
Not just ability.

The Goal Is Maturity—Not Activity

Ephesians 4:13 (NLT)

"This will continue until we all come to such unity... that we will be mature in the Lord..."

The goal of the five-fold ministry is not activity.
It is maturity.
If people are busy but not growing...
Something is off.

The Question You Must Answer

Not:
"Which one do I want to be?"
But:
"Where am I being developed, and how am I growing?"

Closing Thought

The five-fold ministry is not about status.
It is about structure.
It is how God ensures that His church:
Grows
Functions
Stays aligned
And when it operates correctly...
People don't just attend church.
They become equipped.

Real-Life Ministry Scenario

You see a role.

You like how it looks.

You feel drawn to it.

So you start saying:

"I think I'm called to that."

But over time...

You feel:

Out of place

Frustrated

Inconsistent

Because what you were drawn to...

was not what you were designed for.

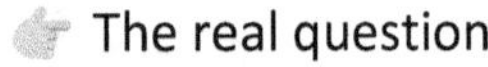 The real question:

Am I called to this... or am I attracted to how it looks?

Self-Evaluation

Be honest:

Am I trying to identify my role—or choose my role?

Do I feel pressure to be something I'm not assigned to?

Am I comparing functions instead of understanding them?

Where am I actually growing right now?

Check Your Heart

Do I want a role... or do I want to be developed?

Have I been chasing titles instead of maturity?

Am I willing to function where I'm needed—not just where I'm seen?

Action Assignment

Study each five-fold role again this week.

Identify which ones you naturally learn from the most.

Ask yourself: where am I being strengthened?

Submit yourself to development—not just desire.

Write and declare:

I will pursue growth over position, and maturity over titles.

Now that you understand:

The structure that equips the house

We move from foundation...

to function on the ground.

Because beyond the five-fold...

there are roles that carry the daily strength of the house.

CHAPTER 8
DEACONS & DEACONESSES
The Strength of Service That Stabilizes the House

If the five-fold ministry is the structure that equips...
Then deacons and deaconesses are the strength that sustains.

You can have:
Powerful preaching
Clear vision
Strong teaching
But without strong service structure...
The house will struggle to function.
Because vision without execution
is just an idea.

This Role Was Created to Solve a Real Problem

> *Acts 6:1–3 (NKJV)*
> *"Now in those days... there arose a complaint... because their widows were neglected... Then the twelve summoned the multitude... and said, 'It is not desirable that we should leave the word of God and serve tables. Therefore... seek out from among you seven men of good reputation, full of the Holy Spirit and wisdom...'"*

Notice the pattern:
There was a problem.
There was a need.
There was potential division.
And instead of ignoring it...
Structure was created to solve it.
Deacons were not created for status.
They were created for stability.

"Serving Tables" Was Never Small

Let's correct this immediately.

When scripture says "serve tables"...

it is not minimizing the role.

It is defining it.

This role is about:

Managing needs

Handling logistics

Maintaining order

Ensuring fairness

Executing what others talk about

Deacons make sure:

What needs to be done... actually gets done.

This Role Protects Focus

The apostles recognized something critical.

If they tried to do everything...

They would lose focus on what they were assigned to do.

So they established a role that would:

Handle practical needs

Maintain order

Ensure care was carried out properly

This is not separation.

This is alignment.

Because when structure is clear...

Everyone can function effectively.

The Qualifications Are Not Casual

Acts 6:3 (NKJV)

"...men of good reputation, full of the Holy Spirit and wisdom..."

Let's break that down.

Good Reputation

Trusted

Consistent

Dependable

Not talented.

Trusted.

Full of the Holy Spirit

Spirit-led

Disciplined

Not reactive

Because serving people requires maturity.

Wisdom

Sound judgment

Discernment

Practical understanding

Because problems are not always simple.

This Role Is About Weight—Not Visibility

Let's deal with the mindset.

This role is not:

About attention

About recognition

About being seen

This role is:

Responsibility without applause

Consistency without spotlight

Execution without constant affirmation

If you need attention to stay consistent…

You are not ready for this role.

You Cannot Be Spiritual and Inconsistent

Let's be direct.

You can:

Pray

Worship

Speak in tongues

Be gifted

And still be:

Unreliable

Disorganized

Inconsistent

Difficult to work with

That does not work here.

Because this role requires:

Dependability

Follow-through

Presence

Stability

Serving Reveals What Preaching Hides

Preaching can be polished.
Serving cannot.

Because serving exposes:
Your attitude
Your patience
Your pride
Your discipline
Your consistency

When you are serving:
There is no stage
No spotlight
No performance
Just responsibility
And your response to it.

Deacons Protect Unity

In Acts 6, the issue was not just food.
It was fairness.
It was care.
It was potential division.
The apostles did not ignore it.
They addressed it with structure.
Deacons ensure:
No group is overlooked
No need is ignored
No issue grows unchecked

They are stabilizers in the house.

Deaconesses Carry the Same Weight

This is not a lesser role.

Deaconesses:

Serve

Support

Lead in execution

Maintain care

With the same expectation of:

Character

Integrity

Faithfulness

This Role Requires Maturity

Because you will:

Handle people

Navigate issues

Solve problems

Carry pressure

Without always having:

Recognition

Affirmation

A platform

You must be able to serve

without being seen.

If You Cannot Be Trusted, You Cannot Be Positioned

Let's connect this back to Chapter 1.

If someone is:

Inconsistent

Unreliable

Unstable

Then they are not ready for this role.

Because this role is built on:

Trust

Faithfulness

Dependability

Not desire.

The Discipline of Finishing What You Start

This role exposes something quickly.

Do you finish what you start?

Or do you:

Start strong

Fade quickly

Disappear when it gets repetitive

Only show up when it is convenient

Because in this role:

Consistency matters more than excitement.

The Question You Must Answer

Not:

"Can I serve?"

But:

"Can I be trusted to carry responsibility consistently?"

Closing Thought

Deacons and deaconesses are not:

Fill-in roles

Backup roles

Entry-level positions

They are:

Structural roles

They hold the house together

in ways most people will never see.

Real-Life Ministry Scenario

You signed up to serve.

At first, you were consistent.

You showed up.

You helped.

You followed through.

But over time...

It became repetitive.

It felt unnoticed.

It started to feel like:

"No one sees what I'm doing."

So you started pulling back.

Not completely.

Just enough that your consistency changed.

👉 The real question:

Did the assignment lose value...

or did your perspective change?

Self-Evaluation

Be honest:

Am I consistent in serving—or conditional?

Do I follow through without being reminded?

Am I dependable when no one is watching?

Do I finish what I start?

If leadership counted on me this week... would I come through?

Check Your Heart

Do I need recognition to stay committed?

Have I allowed repetition to affect my attitude?

Do I serve for impact—or for acknowledgment?

Am I building the house—or just participating in it?

Action Assignment

Choose one area of service this week.

Be fully consistent—no excuses.

Follow through without reminders.

Complete every responsibility assigned to you.

Serve in a way that no one has to check on you.

Write and declare:

I will be faithful in what is unseen, because I understand what I am carrying.

Now that you understand:
The strength of service
The weight of consistency
And the role that stabilizes the house
We now move to those who carry something different.
The Word.
Because speaking for God...
requires more than having something to say.

CHAPTER 9
MINISTERS
& ELDERS

Carriers of the Word and Keepers of the Standard

There is a difference between having something to say…
and being entrusted to speak for God.
Many people can talk.
Few are prepared to carry the weight of the Word.

This Role Is Not Opportunity—It Is Responsibility

Being a minister or an elder is not:
"I get to preach."
"I get to teach."
"I get to be seen."
It is:
"I am responsible for what people believe, understand, and live."
That is weight.

Scripture Sets a Higher Standard

> *James 3:1 (NKJV)*
> *"My brethren, let not many of you become teachers, knowing that we shall receive a stricter judgment."*

Let's not soften that.
Stricter judgment means:
Greater accountability
Higher expectation
Less room for carelessness
When you speak for God…
you will answer to God
for how you handled what you said.

You Don't Just Deliver Messages—You Shape Lives

Every time you:

Preach

Teach

Explain

Lead with the Word

You are shaping:

Perspective

Belief

Behavior

That means:

If you mishandle the Word...

You do not just miss a moment.

You mislead people.

Ministers vs. Elders—Let's Make It Clear

Ministers

Called to communicate the Word

Developing in delivery, understanding, and consistency

Growing in responsibility

Elders

Proven in character and consistency

Trusted to lead, guide, and correct

Carry spiritual oversight and maturity

The difference is not just skill.

It is proven stability over time.

The Word Must First Work on You

Before the Word works through you…

It must work on you.

You do not preach from:

Information

Opinion

Emotion

You preach from:

Transformation

If the Word has not confronted you…

You are not ready to use it to confront others.

Ministry Must Never Contradict the Message

Let's be direct.

You cannot:

Preach discipline and live undisciplined

Preach giving and refuse to give

Preach consistency and be inconsistent

Preach holiness and ignore conviction

That is not a small issue.

That is a credibility issue.

People may hear your words…

But they will follow your patterns.

Preparation Is Not Optional—It Is Respect

2 Timothy 2:15 (NKJV)

"Be diligent to present yourself approved to God...

rightly dividing the word of truth."

Preparation is not:

Last-minute thoughts

Random inspiration

Emotional buildup

Preparation is:

Study

Structure

Clarity

Alignment

Because when you stand to speak...

You are not just sharing ideas.

You are handling truth.

You Do Not Rise to the Moment—You Fall to Your Preparation

Let's correct a myth.

People say:

"When the moment comes, I'll rise."

No you won't.

You will fall to the level of your preparation.

Because pressure does not create discipline.

It exposes it.

How to Prepare Properly

Make it plain.

Study Yourself Full

Know the text.

Context.

Meaning.

Application.

If you do not understand it...

You cannot explain it.

Think Yourself Clear

What are you actually saying?

If you are unclear...

The people will be confused.

Clarity is kindness.

Pray Yourself Hot

You need alignment.

Not performance.

Not hype.

Alignment.

Let Yourself Go

After preparation—

Trust God in the moment.

Do not over-control what you have already prepared.

Know Your Message Before You Speak It

Ask yourself:

What is the purpose of this message?

Is it connected to the text?

What is the main point?

How will people grow from this?

What am I communicating about God?

If you cannot answer these...

You are not ready.

Understand Your Style—and Stay There

Clarity removes confusion.

Expository

Breaking down a specific text in depth

Topical

A theme supported by multiple scriptures

Narrative

Bringing a biblical story to life

Biographical

Studying a biblical character

Inductive

Starting with a question and leading to discovery

Deductive

Starting with truth and proving it

Pick a style.

Stay there.

Do not confuse people trying to do everything at once.

Stage Presence Is Not Performance—It Is Clarity

How you carry yourself matters.

Not for attention.

But for effectiveness.

This includes:

Confidence in delivery

Clear communication

Controlled pacing

Awareness of the room

You do not need to perform.

But you do need to be present.

Do Not Apologize for Being Called

Never step up and say:

"I'm nervous."

"I'm not ready."

"I don't know why they picked me."

That is not humility.

That is a lack of confidence in what God is doing.

Nerves vs. Holy Reverence

Let's make it plain.

Unprepared nerves:

Fear

Confusion

Lack of clarity

Holy reverence:

Awareness

Weight

Dependence on God

When you are prepared...

What you feel is not fear.

It is reverence.

Respect it.

But do not let it control you.

Time Yourself—Respect the Moment

Long does not mean powerful.

Clear does.

Respect:

The moment

The people

The flow

Being effective is more important than being long.

Guard Yourself

This role comes with pressure.

You must guard:

Your time

Your focus

Your discipline

Your mind

Because distractions will dilute what you carry.

Your Life Is Already a Sermon

Before you ever step up to speak...

Your life has already communicated something.

If you had to preach your life right now...

What would it say?

Consistency?

Discipline?

Integrity?

Growth?

Or excuses?

The Question You Must Answer

Not:

"Can I preach?"

But:

"Am I living what I am called to communicate?"

Closing Thought

Being a minister or elder is not about:

Moments

Opportunities

Platforms

It is about:

Carrying truth with integrity, clarity, and consistency.

Real-Life Ministry Scenario

You are asked to preach.

You had time to prepare.

But you delayed.

You assumed:

"I'll flow when I get up there."

Now you are standing in front of people:

Unclear

Scattered

Trying to recover in real time

👉 The real question:

Did you trust God... or neglect preparation and call it faith?

Self-Evaluation

Be honest:

Do I prepare consistently—or only when I feel pressure?

Have I relied on gifting instead of discipline?

Am I clear when I communicate?

Do I understand what I am saying—or just saying something?

Check Your Heart

Do I want opportunities more than I value preparation?

Have I mistaken spontaneity for spirituality?

Am I honoring God with my preparation—or just showing up?

Action Assignment

Identify your primary preaching/teaching style.

Define your preparation process—write it out.

Prepare a message this week fully—no shortcuts.

Practice delivering it.

Eliminate one bad habit (rambling, lack of clarity, over-talking).

Write and declare:

I will honor the Word by preparing to carry it well.

Now that you understand:

The weight of the Word

The responsibility of speaking

And the discipline required to carry it

We now move beyond the walls.

Because some are called to reach what is not yet inside.

CHAPTER 10
EVANGELISTS & MISSIONARIES

The Reach Beyond the Walls

A healthy church does not just grow internally.

It reaches externally.

Because the gospel was never designed to be contained.

It was designed to be carried.

This Is Not Optional—It Is Commanded

Matthew 28:19 (NKJV)

"Go therefore and make disciples of all the nations..."

Jesus did not say:

"Stay comfortable."

"Stay gathered."

"Stay inside."

He said:

GO.

This is not a suggestion.

It is a command.

The Problem: We Have Made Church Inward-Focused

Let's be honest.

Many churches are structured around:

Services

Programs

Internal growth

Member care

And while those things matter...

They are incomplete.

Because when a church only focuses inward...

It slowly becomes:

Comfortable

Predictable

And eventually... stagnant.

Because growth is not just about who stays.

It is about who is being reached.

Evangelism Is Not a Department—It Is a Responsibility

We have reduced evangelism to:

A team

A ministry

A once-a-month effort

But evangelism is not an event.

It is a lifestyle.

Not everyone is called to the office of evangelist.

But everyone is called to reach people.

The Evangelist — The Burden for Souls

2 Timothy 4:5 (NKJV)

"...do the work of an evangelist, fulfill your ministry."

The evangelist carries something different.

Not just passion.

A burden.

A weight for people who are not saved.

They are not satisfied with who is in the room.

They are focused on who is missing.

What Defines an Evangelist

An evangelist:

Sees people differently

Connects quickly

Communicates simply

Feels urgency constantly

They are not driven by attention.

They are driven by:

"Someone needs to be reached."

Evangelists Disrupt Comfort

Let's be honest.

Evangelists make comfortable environments uncomfortable.

Because while others focus on:

Structure

Systems

Internal development

The evangelist is asking:

"Who are we reaching?"

And that question forces the church to confront its focus.

The Missionary — The Sent One

Romans 10:15 (NKJV)

"And how shall they preach unless they are sent?"

While evangelists often move locally…

Missionaries go wherever they are sent.

What Defines a Missionary

A missionary:

Adapts to unfamiliar environments

Carries the message into new spaces

Operates with flexibility and endurance

They are not attached to:

Comfort

Familiarity

Preference

They are committed to:

Assignment.

This Role Requires Sacrifice

Let's remove the romantic version.

Evangelism and missions require:

Rejection

Discomfort

Patience

Persistence

You will:

Be ignored

Be misunderstood

Be dismissed

And still have to show up again.

If You Fear Rejection—You Will Avoid Your Assignment

This is where many people stop.

They need:

Acceptance

Validation

Approval

So they stay silent.

They avoid conversations.

They avoid stepping out.

But reaching people means:

Stepping into spaces where you are not always welcomed.

This Is About People—Not Performance

Evangelism is not:

Scripts

Pressure

Forced conversations

It is:

Relationship

Connection

Authenticity

People do not respond to pressure.

They respond to care.

Your Everyday Life Is Outreach

You do not have to wait for an event.

You reach people:

At work

In conversation

Through your lifestyle

Through your consistency

Before people hear your words…

They observe your life.

Your Life Must Make People Curious

People should be able to look at you and ask:

"What is different about you?"

Not because you are perfect.

But because you are consistent.

Because you are grounded.

Because you carry something real.

If your life does not create curiosity…

Your words will not carry weight.

You Are Not Just Inviting—You Are Interrupting Cycles

When you reach someone…

You are not just saying:

"Come to church."

You are:

Interrupting patterns

Shifting direction

Opening doors

Introducing hope

That is bigger than a conversation.

The Church Must Stay Outward-Focused

A church that only feeds itself…

will eventually fail its assignment.

Because the gospel is not just for those inside.

It is for those who are not here yet.

The Question You Must Answer

Not:

"Am I called to evangelize?"

But:

"Who am I actively reaching?"

Closing Thought

The church does not exist just for those inside it.

It exists for those who are not here yet.

And if we lose that focus...

We lose the heart of the gospel.

Real-Life Ministry Scenario

You see the same people every week.

At work.

In your neighborhood.

In your daily routine.

You talk.

You laugh.

You interact.

But you never go deeper.

You never bring up God.

You never speak life.

You never extend an invitation.

Because you think:

"It's not the right time."

Or:

"I don't want to make it awkward."

So you stay comfortable.

And they stay unchanged.

The real question:

Am I protecting comfort... or fulfilling my assignment?

Self-Evaluation

Be honest:

Who am I actively reaching right now?

Have I allowed fear to silence me?

Do I wait for perfect moments instead of creating them?

Is my life positioned to influence people outside the church?

Check Your Heart

Do I care about people—or just my comfort?

Have I avoided conversations because I fear rejection?

Am I more focused on staying comfortable than being effective?

Action Assignment

Identify one person in your life this week.

Have a real conversation—not surface level.

Share something about your faith.

Extend an invitation.

Do not overthink it.

Be genuine.

Be real.

Write and declare:

I will not stay silent when I have the opportunity to reach.

Now that you understand:
The call to reach beyond the walls
We must return to the center of the house.
Because all of this is held together by one role:
The shepherd.

CHAPTER 11

PASTORS, OVERSEERS & BISHOPS

The Weight of Shepherding and the Responsibility of Souls

There is no role in the house of God
that carries more visible responsibility...
and less understood weight...
than the role of the shepherd.
People see:
The preaching
The platform
The influence
But they do not see:
The pressure
The accountability
The spiritual responsibility

This Role Is Not a Position—It Is a Burden

Jeremiah 3:15 (NKJV)
"And I will give you shepherds according to My heart,
who will feed you with knowledge and understanding."

God does not just appoint pastors.
He entrusts them.
Because at the center of this role...
are people.

A Shepherd Is Responsible for Souls

Hebrews 13:17 (NKJV)
"...for they watch out for your souls, as those who must
give account..."

Let that sit.

A shepherd will answer to God for:

What was taught

How people were led

What was allowed

What was corrected

That is not light.

That is weight.

This Is Not About Popularity

A true shepherd is not driven by:

Applause

Approval

Public opinion

Because if you lead based on what people want...

You will fail them spiritually.

The Role of a Shepherd

A shepherd:

Feeds

Protects

Guides

Corrects

Feeds

Delivers the Word with clarity and consistency.

Protects

Guards the house from:

False doctrine

Harmful influence

Spiritual danger

Guides

Provides direction for:

The vision

The house

The people

Corrects

Addresses what is:

Out of order

Misaligned

Harmful

Even when it is uncomfortable.

Correction Is Not Rejection

This is where people struggle.

They hear correction…

and feel attacked.

They are adjusted…

and feel rejected.

But correction is not rejection.

It is care.

A shepherd that never corrects...

is not protecting the sheep.

Overseer & Bishop — Expanded Responsibility

These are not different in nature.

They are expanded in scope.

Overseer

Responsible for systems and structure

Ensures order is maintained

Provides leadership beyond one function

Bishop

Carries spiritual authority over a broader scope

Establishes doctrine and direction

Oversees leadership development

The weight increases.

Not just the title.

You Cannot Shepherd Without Sacrifice

Let's remove the illusion.

This role will cost you:

Time

Energy

Privacy

Emotional capacity

You will:

Carry people's burdens

Navigate difficult situations

Make decisions not everyone agrees with

And still have to lead.

You Must Lead Even When Misunderstood

There will be moments when:

People question your decisions

People disagree with your direction

People do not understand your reasoning

And you still have to lead.

Because leadership is not validated by agreement.

It is proven by responsibility.

You Cannot Be Controlled by People

If a shepherd is led by:

Opinions

Emotions

Pressure

They will compromise the vision.

Vision flows from God

through leadership

to the house.

Not through group opinion.

Honor Is Not Optional

1 Thessalonians 5:12–13 (NKJV)

"...recognize those who labor among you... esteem them very highly in love for their work's sake..."

Honor is not about personality.
It is about responsibility.
It is about recognizing the weight someone carries.

The Danger of Dishonor

Dishonor:
Disrupts order
Creates division
Weakens structure
Because when leadership is constantly questioned publicly...
The house becomes unstable.

Shepherds Must Also Be Accountable

Let's balance this.
Leadership is not above accountability.
Shepherds must:
Remain submitted to God
Remain aligned with truth
Remain consistent in character
Authority without accountability
becomes abuse.

A Shepherd Must Have a Heart for People

This is not just:

Strategy

Systems

Leadership

This is:

Care

Because you are not leading programs.

You are leading people.

You Cannot Shepherd from a Distance

This role requires:

Presence

Awareness

Engagement

Because people need:

Guidance

Covering

Connection

Not just instruction.

The Question You Must Answer

Not:

"Do I want this role?"

But:

"Am I willing to carry the weight that comes with it?"

Closing Thought

Shepherding is not glamorous.

It is costly.

But it is one of the most sacred responsibilities

in the Kingdom of God.

Because at the center of it all...

are people.

Real-Life Ministry Scenario

You disagree with a decision.

You do not have full context.

You do not understand the reasoning.

But instead of seeking clarity...

You begin to question.

You talk to others.

You form opinions.

You create narratives.

And without realizing it...

You are weakening what you are supposed to be supporting.

👉 The real question:

Am I seeking understanding... or spreading confusion?

Self-Evaluation

Be honest:

Do I trust the leadership God has placed over me?

Do I seek clarity—or assume the worst?

Am I strengthening the house—or creating tension?

Do I understand the weight leadership carries?

Check Your Heart

Do I honor leadership—or critique it internally?

Have I allowed disagreement to turn into dishonor?

Do I respect the responsibility leaders carry?

Action Assignment

If you do not understand something—ask, don't assume.

Choose honor in how you speak about leadership.

Pray for your leaders this week intentionally.

Write and declare:

I will honor what I may not fully understand, because I respect the weight it carries.

Now that you understand:

The weight of shepherding

The responsibility of leadership

And the role that carries the house

We now bring it back to you.

Because understanding roles means nothing

if you do not understand where you fit.

CHAPTER 12

FINDING YOUR PLACE

Clarity, Commitment, and Moving With Intention

You have now:

Heard the truth

Understood the structure

Seen the roles

Felt the weight

But none of that matters...

if you still do not know where you fit.

Because understanding without movement

creates stagnation.

The Danger of Staying Undefined

Many people stay in church environments for years...

Attending

Listening

Agreeing

But never defining their place.

They are present...

but not positioned.

And when you are not positioned...

you become passive.

You observe more than you contribute.

You consume more than you build.

You agree more than you act.

You Were Never Meant to Just Attend

Let's make this clear.

You were not saved to sit.

You were not called to spectate.

You were not brought into the house
just to receive.
You were brought in
to function.

Your Place Is Discovered Through Movement

Here's where many people get stuck.
They are waiting to "figure it out"
before they move.
But clarity does not come from waiting.
It comes from serving.
It comes from trying.
It comes from showing up.
You discover your place
by engaging—not by analyzing.

You Will Not Get It Perfect Immediately

Let's remove pressure.
You may not land in the perfect role immediately.
You may:
Try something
Adjust
Grow
Refine
That is part of the process.
What matters is not perfection.
It is participation.

Comparison Will Confuse You

If you measure your place by someone else's position...

You will always feel off.

Because you were not designed to duplicate.

You were designed to function.

Comparison leads to:

Frustration

Delay

Misalignment

Clarity comes from:

Understanding who you are

and where you are needed.

Your Place Will Always Be Connected to Need

This is key.

Your place is not just about what you want to do.

It is about what the house needs.

Because purpose is not:

Self-focused

It is:

Service-focused.

When you shift from:

"What do I want?"

To:

"What is needed?"

You move into alignment.

Faithfulness Reveals Placement

Let's bring it full circle.

You do not prove your place

by claiming it.

You reveal your place

through consistency.

When you:

Show up

Serve well

Stay consistent

Handle responsibility

Your placement becomes clear over time.

You Cannot Grow Without Commitment

This is where many people stop.

They want clarity...

without commitment.

They want growth...

without consistency.

But growth requires:

Showing up repeatedly

Serving consistently

Staying planted

You cannot develop

if you are always moving.

Stop Waiting to Be Picked

This is the mindset shift.

You are not waiting to be chosen.

You are choosing to respond.

Because waiting creates passivity.

But responding creates movement.

Your Role May Not Be Visible—But It Is Valuable

Let's confront this directly.

If you only value visible roles...

You will miss your place.

Because some of the most important functions:

Are not seen

Are not celebrated

Are not platformed

But they are necessary.

The House Needs You Functioning

Not guessing

Not comparing

Not waiting

Functioning.

Because when every part works:

The house grows

The vision moves

People are impacted

The Question You Must Answer

Not:

"Where do I want to be?"

But:

"Where am I willing to commit and grow?"

Closing Thought

Finding your place is not about:

Feeling ready

Being perfect

Having everything figured out

It is about:

Responding

Serving

Staying consistent

And allowing God to make it clear over time.

Real-Life Ministry Scenario

You've been in the house.

You've heard the teaching.

You've felt the conviction.

You know you should be doing more.

But you keep saying:

"I'm still figuring it out."

Meanwhile:

Opportunities pass

Needs go unmet

Time keeps moving

And you remain in the same place.

👉 The real question:

Am I truly searching for clarity…

or avoiding commitment?

Self-Evaluation

Be honest:

Am I actively serving—or just attending?

Have I committed anywhere consistently?

Do I follow through—or fade out?

Am I waiting for clarity instead of engaging?

Check Your Heart

Am I avoiding responsibility?

Do I fear committing to something long-term?

Have I allowed comparison to keep me stuck?

Do I value comfort over growth?

Action Assignment

Choose one area to serve consistently.

Commit to it fully for the next 30 days.

Show up, follow through, and stay present.

Ask for feedback and grow from it.

Write and declare:

I will not stay undefined. I will commit, serve, and grow into my place.

FINAL CHARGE

Now What Will You Do?

You've read it.
You've seen it.
You've felt it.
Now we have to deal with the only thing that actually matters:
What are you going to do about it?

At this point, you don't lack knowledge. You know what faithfulness requires. You understand what serving exposes. You've seen what calling demands. You've been shown how structure works, what leadership carries, and what outreach requires.

So now the tension has shifted.
It's no longer, *"I didn't know."*
Now it's, *"I know... and I have to respond."*
And that's where most people stop.
They feel it.
They agree with it.
They even say, "That's good."
But agreement has never changed anyone.
Agreement feels right—but it doesn't move anything.
Action does.
This is the moment where people decide who they're going to be.

Some will close this book, feel inspired, and go right back to the same habits, the same inconsistency, the same patterns they've been living in. And over time, what once felt like conviction will fade into memory.

Don't let that be you.
Because this moment—right here—is not about a title, a platform, or an opportunity.
It's about a decision.
A decision to be consistent when it's inconvenient.
A decision to be accountable when no one is watching.
A decision to align when it would be easier to stay comfortable.
A decision to take responsibility instead of waiting for recognition.

You don't need another confirmation.
You don't need another moment.
You don't need someone to notice you or pick you.
You already know enough to move.
And if you're honest, you already know where.
There's an area where you've been inconsistent.
There's a place where you've been passive.
There's a responsibility you've been delaying.
There's a step you've been avoiding.
And now you don't have the excuse of uncertainty anymore.
So don't leave this vague. Don't leave this emotional. Don't leave this as a moment that fades.
Make it real.
Decide where you will serve.
Decide what you will commit to.
Decide what changes today—not next week, not when things slow down, but now.
Because this is bigger than you.

This is about the people connected to your life. The people who will be influenced by your consistency. The people who will benefit from your obedience. The people who will miss out if you stay stagnant.

Your growth is not isolated.

And neither is your delay.

So don't walk away from this saying, *"That was powerful."*

Walk away saying, *"I'm different now."*

Not because you felt something...

But because you decided something.

Decided that faithfulness is not optional.

Decided that serving is not seasonal.

Decided that growth is not accidental.

Decided that alignment matters.

Decided that responsibility is yours.

This is your moment.

Not to agree.

But to move.

And the only question left is not what you learned...

It's what you're about to do differently—starting now.

BONUS SECTION

TOOLS TO STRENGTHEN YOUR FOUNDATION

You Cannot Grow Without the Word

Everything in this book points back to one thing:

The Word of God.

You can be:

- consistent
- committed
- serving

But if you are not grounded in the Word...

You will eventually become:

- unstable
- unclear
- easily influenced

Because growth in God is not sustained by emotion.

It is sustained by truth.

Understanding the Bible (Simple Framework)

The Bible is not random.

It is structured.

Old Testament (Foundation)

Books of the Law (Genesis–Deuteronomy)

The beginning. Creation, covenant, and God establishing His people.

Historical Books (Joshua–Esther)

The story of Israel—victories, failures, leadership, and lessons.

Wisdom & Poetry (Job–Song of Solomon)

Practical life, worship, and emotional honesty before God.

The Prophets (Isaiah–Malachi)

Correction, warning, and the call back to alignment with God.

New Testament (Fulfillment & Function)

The Gospels (Matthew–John)

The life, teachings, and mission of Jesus Christ.

Acts of the Apostles

The birth and expansion of the early church.

Pauline Letters (Romans–Philemon)

Instruction, correction, and doctrine for the church.

General Epistles (Hebrews–Jude)

Encouragement, warning, and spiritual growth.

Revelation

Prophecy, fulfillment, and the ultimate victory of Christ.

The Word Is Your Weapon

Ephesians 6:17 calls the Word of God:

"the sword of the Spirit."

That means:

- you don't just read it
- you use it

The Word:

- corrects you
- strengthens you
- stabilizes you
- equips you

Without it, you will rely on:

- feelings
- opinions
- culture

And those are unstable foundations.

How to Approach the Word Properly

1. Hermeneutics — Interpreting the Word

This simply means:

Understanding what the text actually means.

Ask:

- Who is speaking?
- Who are they speaking to?
- What is the context?
- What is the principle?

Don't just read to feel something.

Read to understand something.

2. Theology — Understanding the Word

This is:

Knowing what you believe—and why.

Not based on:

- trends
- opinions
- social media

But based on:

- scripture
- truth

- consistency

If you don't know what you believe…

You will believe anything

3. Homiletics — Communicating the Word

For those called to teach or preach:

This is:

Preparing to communicate clearly and correctly.

It's not about:

- sounding good
- being impressive

It's about:

- being accurate
- being clear
- being effective

Simple Daily Approach

You don't need to overcomplicate this.

Start with:

- One passage
- One focus
- One application

Ask:

- What is this saying?
- What does it mean?
- How do I apply it today?

Consistency matters more than volume.

You will not outgrow your need for the Word.

No matter your role:

- servant
- leader
- minister
- pastor

The Word remains your foundation.

Your Responsibility

Don't just read this section and move on.

Start building your discipline now.

Because everything you become in God...

Will be sustained by what you know and live from His Word.

About the Author

Pastor Erick D. Bowens is a pastor, leadership developer, and creative strategist committed to developing people through clarity, structure, and intentional growth.

With years of experience serving in ministry at multiple levels, he has built his approach on one foundational principle: faithfulness before visibility. His leadership is shaped by hands-on service, real-world responsibility, and the discipline of aligning calling with consistency.

As a pastor and mentor, he focuses on helping individuals move beyond passive belief into active responsibility—equipping them to serve effectively, lead with integrity, and function within the structure of the Kingdom.

Through his work in ministry and business, Pastor Erick continues to develop systems, training, and resources that challenge people to grow, align, and move with purpose.

"Connect with Pastor Erick for leadership training, ministry development, and creative strategy."

Connect: (903) – 866 - 7670

info@bowensenterprise.org or

pastorerick@betheltemplelongview.org

www.ingramcontent.com/pod-product-compliance
Lightning Source LLC
LaVergne TN
LVHW010922110826
845149LV00013B/2447